Reading: Literature Learning Stations Grades 6–8
English Language Arts series

Authors:	Schyrlet Cameron and Suzanne Myers
Editors:	Mary Dieterich and Sarah M. Anderson
Proofreader:	Margaret Brown

COPYRIGHT © 2013 Mark Twain Media, Inc.

ISBN 978-1-62223-002-0

Printing No. CD-404177

Mark Twain Media, Inc., Publishers
Distributed by Carson-Dellosa Publishing LLC

Visit us at www.carsondellosa.com

Table of Contents

To the Teacher

In the *English Language Arts* (ELA) series, students in grades six through eight explore reading, writing, and language in a learning station environment. Learning stations engage students in individual or small group activities. Learning stations are an instructional strategy that can be used to target specific skills.

Each book in the ELA series features five or six units of study. Each unit has a teacher page that identifies the goal, states the standards, lists materials and setup for the activities, and provides instructions to be presented to students. Also, there are questions for opening discussion and student reflection. (Note: It is important for the teacher to introduce, model, or review the concepts or skills with the students at the beginning of each unit.)

Books in the ELA Series

- *Reading: Literature Learning Stations, Grades 6–8*
  The units focus on alliteration, rhyme, plot and setting, tone and mood, and poetry.

- *Reading: Informational Text Learning Stations, Grades 6–8*
  The units focus on citing evidence, bias, point of view, propaganda techniques, organizational text structures, and text features.

- *Writing Learning Stations, Grades 6–8*
  The units focus on fact and opinion, characterization, making inferences, proofreading, and dialogue.

- *Language Learning Stations, Grades 6–8*
  The units focus on punctuation, dictionary usage, figurative language, roots and affixes, and word meaning.

Reading: Literature Learning Stations, Grades 6–8, contains five units of study. Each unit consists of four to five learning station activities. The activity at each station is designed to create interest, provide practice, and stimulate discussion. These units will help students become better readers of literature and poetry as they learn to cite evidence from the text and become aware of point of view; alliteration and rhyme; plot, setting, and characters; and other literary devices. Whenever applicable, media/technology and speaking/listening skills are integrated into the activity. Handouts are provided as supplemental resources.

The units of study in the ELA series are meant to supplement or enhance the regular classroom English Language Arts curriculum. The station activities are correlated to the strands of the English Language Arts Common Core State Standards.

Common Core State Standards Matrix

English Language Arts Standards: Reading Literature

Units of Study	RL.6.1	RL.6.2	RL.6.3	RL.6.4	RL.6.5	RL.6.6	RL.6.7	RL.6.8	RL.6.9	RL.6.10	RL.7.1	RL.7.2	RL.7.3	RL.7.4	RL.7.5	RL.7.6	RL.7.7	RL.7.8	RL.7.9	RL.7.10	RL.8.1	RL.8.2	RL.8.3	RL.8.4	RL.8.5	RL.8.6	RL.8.7	RL.8.8	RL.8.9	RL.8.10
Literature: Inferences & Evidence	X										X										X									
Plot, Setting, and Character			X										X										X							
Alliteration and Rhyme				X										X										X						
Point of View						X										X										X				
Poetry									X										X										X	

Teacher Page

Unit: Literature: Inferences and Evidence

Goal: Students will be able to make inferences from literature and cite textual evidence to support their inferences.

Common Core State Standards (CCSS):

6th Grade	7th Grade	8th Grade
RL.6.1. Cite textual evidence to support analysis of what the text says explicitly as well as inferences drawn from the text.	RL.7.1. Cite several pieces of textual evidence to support analysis of what the text says explicitly as well as inferences drawn from the text.	RL.8.1. Cite the textual evidence that most strongly supports an analysis of what the text says explicitly as well as inferences drawn from the text.

© Copyright 2010. National Governors Association Center for Best Practices and Council of Chief State School Officers. All rights reserved.

Materials List/Setup

Station 1: Finding Evidence (Activity); Passage One (Handout)
Station 2: Analyzing Text (Activity); Passage Two (Handout)
Station 3: Making a Comparison (Activity); Passage Three (Handout)
Station 4: Making Inferences (Activity); Passage Four (Handout)
Station 5: Citing Textual Evidence (Activity); Passage Five (Handout)

Activity: one copy per student
Handout: one copy per each student in a group

Opening: Discussion Questions (Teacher-Directed)

1. How many of you have a dog as a pet?
2. How did you acquire the dog?
3. What actions express your level of devotion toward the dog and the dog toward you?
4. Do you think your dog loves you, or is it just being loyal?

Student Instructions for Learning Stations

At the learning stations, you will read passages taken from the classic novel *The Call of the Wild* by Jack London. After reading each passage, you will analyze the passage, make inferences, and support your inferences by citing textual evidence. Discuss your answers with other team members after completing each activity.

Closure: Reflection

The following questions can be used to stimulate discussion or as a journaling activity.
1. Is *The Call of the Wild* an appropriate title for this book?
2. How is Buck's life with Judge Miller different from his life with John Thornton?
3. How does Buck's response to "the call of the wild" change over time?

Name: _____   Date: _____

Station One: Finding Evidence

Directions: Read Passage One, an excerpt from *The Call of the Wild* by Jack London. In the first column are statements about the passage. From the passage, cite evidence that supports each statement.

Statement	**Evidence**

1. In this passage, Jack London used the literary device of foreshadowing. ←

2. Buck's life as a dog was easy at Judge Miller's place. ←

3. Judge Miller, Buck's first owner, was a wealthy man. ←

4. Buck was a mixed-breed dog. ←

Name: _____ Date: _____

Station Two: Analyzing Text

Directions: Read Passage Two, an excerpt from *The Call of the Wild* by Jack London. Answer each question below and cite textual evidence that supports your answer. The answer to each question is either explicitly stated in the passage, or you will need to make an inference.

Question	Answer
1. What relation was Mercedes to Hal?	
2. Did Hal and Charles follow Mercedes' advice about packing the sled?	
3. What was the condition of his new owner's campsite?	
4. What was the condition of Buck and the other dogs before beginning the trip?	
5. How did Charles and Hal's inexperience affect the trip?	

Name: _____ Date: _____

Station Three: Making a Comparison

Directions: Read Passage Three, an excerpt from *The Call of the Wild* by Jack London. Use the T-Chart to compare the ways John Thornton and Buck showed their love or devotion toward each other. Then answer the question below.

1.

John Thornton	Buck

2. How did Buck's love of John Thornton differ from the love John Thornton had for Buck? Cite textual evidence to support your answer.

_____

_____

_____

_____

_____

_____

Name: _____   Date: _____

Station Four: Making Inferences

Directions: Read Passage Four, an excerpt from *The Call of the Wild* by Jack London. Answer the following questions. Cite textual evidence to support your answers.

1. How did the call from "the depths of the forest" affect Buck?

_____

_____

_____

_____

_____

2. Why did Buck want to befriend the wolf?

_____

_____

_____

_____

_____

_____

_____

3. What was Buck's internal conflict?

_____

_____

_____

_____

_____

_____

Station Five: Citing Textual Evidence

Directions: Read Passage Five, an excerpt from *The Call of the Wild* by Jack London. Answer each question and cite the best textual evidence that supports your answer.

1. How did Buck know John Thornton was dead?

_____

_____

_____

_____

_____

_____

2. Why was Buck "as never before" ready to obey the call?

_____

_____

_____

_____

_____

_____

3. What were Buck's final two actions that completed his acceptance of the call?

_____

_____

_____

_____

_____

_____

_____

Passage One: *The Call of the Wild*

Buck did not read the newspapers, or he would have known that trouble was brewing, not alone for himself, but for every tide-water dog, strong of muscle and with warm, long hair, from Puget Sound to San Diego. Because men, groping in the Arctic darkness, had found a yellow metal, and . . . thousands of men were rushing into the Northland. These men wanted dogs, and the dogs they wanted were heavy dogs, with strong muscles by which to toil, and furry coats to protect them from the frost.

Buck lived at a big house in the sun-kissed Santa Clara Valley. Judge Miller's place, it was called. It stood back from the road, half hidden among the trees, through which glimpses could be caught of the wide cool veranda that ran around its four sides. The house was approached by gravelled driveways which wound about through wide-spreading lawns and under the interlacing boughs of tall poplars. At the rear things were on even a more spacious scale than at the front. There were great stables . . . rows of vine-clad servants' cottages, an endless and orderly array of outhouses, long grape arbors, green pastures, orchards, and berry patches. Then there was the pumping plant for the artesian well, and the big cement tank where Judge Miller's boys took their morning plunge and kept cool in the hot afternoon.

And over this great demesne Buck ruled. Here he was born, and here he had lived the four years of his life. It was true, there were other dogs. There could not but be other dogs on so vast a place, but they did not count. They came and went, resided in the populous kennels, or lived obscurely in the recesses of the house . . .

But Buck was neither house-dog nor kennel-dog. The whole realm was his. He plunged into the swimming tank or went hunting with the Judge's sons; he escorted Mollie and Alice, the Judge's daughters, on long twilight or early morning rambles; on wintry nights he lay at the Judge's feet before the roaring library fire; he carried the Judge's grandsons on his back, or rolled them in the grass, and guarded their footsteps through wild adventures down to the fountain in the stable yard, and even beyond, where the paddocks were, and the berry patches. Among the terriers he stalked imperiously, and Toots and Ysabel he utterly ignored, for he was king—king over all creeping, crawling, flying things of Judge Miller's place, humans included.

His father, Elmo, a huge St. Bernard, had been the Judge's inseparable companion, and Buck bid fair to follow in the way of his father. He was not so large—he weighed only one hundred and forty pounds—for his mother, Shep, had been a Scotch shepherd dog. Nevertheless, one hundred and forty pounds, to which was added the dignity that comes of good living and universal respect, enabled him to carry himself in right royal fashion. During the four years since his puppyhood he had lived the life of a sated aristocrat; he had a fine pride in himself, was even a trifle egotistical, as country gentlemen sometimes become because of their insular situation. But he had saved himself by not becoming a mere pampered house-dog. Hunting and kindred outdoor delights had kept down the fat and hardened his muscles; and to him, as to the cold-tubbing races, the love of water had been a tonic and a health preserver.

And this was the manner of dog Buck was in the fall of 1897, when the Klondike strike dragged men from all the world into the frozen North. . .

(Excerpt from *The Call of the Wild* by Jack London)

Passage Two: *The Call of the Wild*

Three days passed, by which time Buck and his mates found how really tired and weak they were. Then, on the morning of the fourth day, two men from the States came along and bought them, harness and all, for a song. The men addressed each other as "Hal" and "Charles" . . . Both men were manifestly out of place, and why such as they should adventure the North is part of the mystery of things that passes understanding.

. . . When driven with his mates to the new owners' camp, Buck saw a slipshod and slovenly affair, tent half stretched, dishes unwashed, everything in disorder; also, he saw a woman. "Mercedes" the men called her. She was Charles's wife and Hal's sister—a nice family party.

Buck watched them apprehensively as they proceeded to take down the tent and load the sled. There was a great deal of effort about their manner, but no businesslike method. The tent was rolled into an awkward bundle three times as large as it should have been. The tin dishes were packed away unwashed. Mercedes continually fluttered in the way of her men and kept up an unbroken chattering of remonstrance and advice. When they put a clothes-sack on the front of the sled, she suggested it should go on the back; and when they had put it on the back, and covered it over with a couple of other bundles, she discovered overlooked articles which could abide nowhere else but in that very sack, and they unloaded again . . .

Late next morning Buck led the long team up the street. There was nothing lively about it, no snap or go in him and his fellows. They were starting dead weary. Four times he had covered the distance between Salt Water and Dawson, and the knowledge that, jaded and tired, he was facing the same trail once more, made him bitter. His heart was not in the work, nor was the heart of any dog . . .

Buck felt vaguely that there was no depending upon these two men and the woman. They did not know how to do anything, and as the days went by it became apparent that they could not learn. They were slack in all things, without order or discipline. It took them half the night to pitch a slovenly camp, and half the morning to break that camp and get the sled loaded in fashion so slovenly that for the rest of the day they were occupied in stopping and rearranging the load. Some days they did not make ten miles. On other days they were unable to get started at all. And on no day did they succeed in making more than half the distance used by the men as a basis in their dog-food computation.

It was inevitable that they should go short on dog food. But they hastened it by overfeeding, bringing the day nearer when underfeeding would commence . . . But it was not food that Buck and the huskies needed, but rest. And though they were making poor time, the heavy load they dragged sapped their strength severely.

(Excerpt from *The Call of the Wild* by Jack London)

Passage Three: *The Call of the Wild*

To Buck's surprise these dogs manifested no jealousy toward him. They seemed to share the kindliness and largeness of John Thornton. As Buck grew stronger they enticed him into all sorts of ridiculous games, in which Thornton himself could not forbear to join; and in this fashion Buck romped through his convalescence and into a new existence. Love, genuine passionate love, was his for the first time. This he had never experienced at Judge Miller's down in the sun-kissed Santa Clara Valley. With the Judge's sons, hunting and tramping, it had been a working partnership; with the Judge's grandsons, a sort of pompous guardianship; and with the Judge himself, a stately and dignified friendship. But love that was feverish and burning, that was adoration, that was madness, it had taken John Thornton to arouse.

This man had saved his life, which was something; but, further, he was the ideal master. Other men saw to the welfare of their dogs from a sense of duty and business expediency; he saw to the welfare of his as if they were his own children, because he could not help it. And he saw further. He never forgot a kindly greeting or a cheering word, and to sit down for a long talk with them ("gas" he called it) was as much his delight as theirs. He had a way of taking Buck's head roughly between his hands, and resting his own head upon Buck's, of shaking him back and forth, the while calling him ill names that to Buck were love names. Buck knew no greater joy than that rough embrace and the sound of murmured oaths, and at each jerk back and forth it seemed that his heart would be shaken out of his body so great was its ecstasy . . .

For the most part, however, Buck's love was expressed in adoration. While he went wild with happiness when Thornton touched him or spoke to him, he did not seek these tokens . . . Buck was content to adore at a distance. He would lie by the hour, eager, alert, at Thornton's feet, looking up into his face, dwelling upon it, studying it, following with keenest interest each fleeting expression, every movement or change of feature. Or, as chance might have it, he would lie farther away, to the side or rear, watching the outlines of the man and the occasional movements of his body. And often, such was the communion in which they lived, the strength of Buck's gaze would draw John Thornton's head around, and he would return the gaze, without speech, his heart shining out of his eyes as Buck's heart shone out.

For a long time after his rescue, Buck did not like Thornton to get out of his sight. From the moment he left the tent to when he entered it again, Buck would follow at his heels. His transient masters since he had come into the Northland had bred in him a fear that no master could be permanent. He was afraid that Thornton would pass out of his life as Perrault and Francois and the Scotch half-breed had passed out. . . .

But in spite of this great love he bore John Thornton, which seemed to bespeak the soft civilizing influence, the strain of the primitive, which the Northland had aroused in him, remained alive and active. Faithfulness and devotion, things born of fire and roof, were his; yet he retained his wildness and wiliness. He was a thing of the wild, come in from the wild to sit by John Thornton's fire, rather than a dog of the soft Southland stamped with the marks of generations of civilization. Because of his very great love, he could not steal from this man, but from any other man, in any other camp, he did not hesitate an instant; while the cunning with which he stole enabled him to escape detection.

(Excerpt from *The Call of the Wild* by Jack London)

Passage Four: *The Call of the Wild*

And closely akin to the visions of the hairy man was the call still sounding in the depths of the forest. It filled him with a great unrest and strange desires. It caused him to feel a vague, sweet gladness, and he was aware of wild yearnings and stirrings for he knew not what. Sometimes he pursued the call into the forest, looking for it as though it were a tangible thing, barking softly or defiantly, as the mood might dictate . . .

One night he sprang from sleep with a start. From the forest came the call . . . distinct and definite as never before,—a long-drawn howl, like, yet unlike, any noise made by husky dog. And he knew it, in the old familiar way, as a sound heard before. He sprang through the sleeping camp and in swift silence dashed through the woods. As he drew closer to the cry he went more slowly, with caution in every movement, till he came to an open place among the trees, and looking out saw, erect on haunches, with nose pointed to the sky, a long, lean timber wolf.

He had made no noise, yet it ceased from its howling and tried to sense his presence. Buck stalked into the open, half crouching, body gathered compactly together, tail straight and stiff, feet falling with unwonted care. Every movement advertised commingled threatening and overture of friendliness . . . But the wolf fled at sight of him. He followed, with wild leapings, in a frenzy to overtake. He ran him into a blind channel, in the bed of the creek where a timber jam barred the way. The wolf whirled about, pivoting on his hind legs . . . snarling and bristling, clipping his teeth together in a continuous and rapid succession of snaps.

Buck did not attack, but circled him about and hedged him in with friendly advances. The wolf was suspicious and afraid; for Buck made three of him in weight, while his head barely reached Buck's shoulder. Watching his chance, he darted away, and the chase was resumed . . .

But in the end Buck's pertinacity was rewarded; for the wolf, finding that no harm was intended, finally sniffed noses with him. Then they became friendly, and played about in the nervous, half-coy way with which fierce beasts belie their fierceness. After some time of this the wolf started off at an easy lope in a manner that plainly showed he was going somewhere. He made it clear to Buck that he was to come, and they ran side by side . . .

They stopped by a running stream to drink, and, stopping, Buck remembered John Thornton. He sat down. The wolf started on toward the place from where the call surely came, then returned to him, sniffing noses and making actions as though to encourage him. But Buck turned about and started slowly on the back track. For the better part of an hour the wild brother ran by his side, whining softly. Then he sat down, pointed his nose upward, and howled. It was a mournful howl, and as Buck held steadily on his way he heard it grow faint and fainter until it was lost in the distance.

John Thornton was eating dinner when Buck dashed into camp and sprang upon him in a frenzy of affection, overturning him, scrambling upon him, licking his face, biting his hand— "playing the general tom-fool," as John Thornton characterized it, the while he shook Buck back and forth and cursed him lovingly.

For two days and nights Buck never left camp, never let Thornton out of his sight . . . But after two days the call in the forest began to sound more imperiously than ever . . . Once again he took to wandering in the woods, but the wild brother came no more; and though he listened through long vigils, the mournful howl was never raised.

(Excerpt from *The Call of the Wild* by Jack London)

Passage Five: *The Call of the Wild*

And truly Buck was the Fiend incarnate, raging at their heels and dragging them down like deer as they raced through the trees. It was a fateful day for the Yeehats . . . As for Buck, wearying of the pursuit, he returned to the desolated camp. He found Pete where he had been killed in his blankets in the first moment of surprise. Thornton's desperate struggle was fresh-written on the earth, and Buck scented every detail of it down to the edge of a deep pool . . . The pool itself, muddy and discolored from the sluice boxes, effectually hid what it contained, and it contained John Thornton; for Buck followed his trace into the water, from which no trace led away.

All day Buck brooded by the pool or roamed restlessly about the camp. Death, as a cessation of movement, as a passing out and away from the lives of the living, he knew, and he knew John Thornton was dead. It left a great void in him, somewhat akin to hunger, but a void which ached and ached, and which food could not fill . . .

Night came on, and a full moon rose high over the trees into the sky, lighting the land till it lay bathed in ghostly day. And with the coming of the night, brooding and mourning by the pool, Buck became alive to a stirring of the new life in the forest other than that which the Yeehats had made. He stood up, listening and scenting. From far away drifted a faint, sharp yelp, followed by a chorus of similar sharp yelps. As the moments passed the yelps grew closer and louder. Again Buck knew them as things heard in that other world which persisted in his memory. He walked to the centre of the open space and listened. It was the call, the many-noted call, sounding more luringly and compellingly than ever before. And as never before, he was ready to obey. John Thornton was dead. The last tie was broken. Man and the claims of man no longer bound him.

. . . the wolf pack had at last crossed over from the land of streams and timber and invaded Buck's valley. Into the clearing where the moonlight streamed, they poured in a silvery flood; and in the centre of the clearing stood Buck, motionless as a statue, waiting their coming. They were awed, so still and large he stood, and a moment's pause fell, till the boldest one leaped straight for him . . . Three others tried it in sharp succession; and one after the other they drew back, streaming blood from slashed throats or shoulders . . .

. . . at the end of half an hour the wolves drew back discomfited. The tongues of all were out and lolling, the white fangs showing cruelly white in the moonlight. Some were lying down with heads raised and ears pricked forward; others stood on their feet, watching him; and still others were lapping water from the pool. One wolf, long and lean and gray, advanced cautiously, in a friendly manner, and Buck recognized the wild brother with whom he had run for a night and a day. He was whining softly, and, as Buck whined, they touched noses.

Then an old wolf, gaunt and battle-scarred, came forward. Buck writhed his lips into the preliminary of a snarl, but sniffed noses with him, Whereupon the old wolf sat down, pointed nose at the moon, and broke out the long wolf howl. The others sat down and howled. And now the call came to Buck in unmistakable accents. He, too, sat down and howled. This over, he came out of his angle and the pack crowded around him, sniffing in half-friendly, half-savage manner. The leaders lifted the yelp of the pack and sprang away into the woods. The wolves swung in behind, yelping in chorus. And Buck ran with them, side by side with the wild brother, yelping as he ran.

(Excerpt from *The Call of the Wild* by Jack London)

Teacher Page

Unit: Plot, Setting, and Character

Goal: Students will be able to analyze the role of plot devices: setting, sequenced events, characters, and dialogue.

Common Core State Standards (CCSS):

6th Grade	7th Grade	8th Grade
RL.6.3. Describe how a particular story's or drama's plot unfolds in a series of episodes as well as how the characters respond or change as the plot moves toward a resolution.	RL.7.3. Analyze how particular elements of a story or drama interact (e.g., how setting shapes the characters or plot).	RL.8.3. Analyze how particular lines of dialogue or incidents in a story or drama propel the action, reveal aspects of character, or provoke a decision.

© Copyright 2010. National Governors Association Center for Best Practices and Council of Chief State School Officers. All rights reserved.

Materials List/Setup

Station 1: Plot (Activity); *Little Red Riding Hood* (Handout)
Station 2: Character Traits (Activity); Examples of Character Traits (Handout); *Little Red Riding Hood* (Handout)
Station 3: Character Types (Activity); *Little Red Riding Hood* (Handout)
Station 4: Analyzing Dialogue (Activity)

Activity: one copy per student
Handout: one copy per each student in a group

Opening Activity and Discussion Questions (Teacher-Directed)

1. Have you ever judged someone based on a first impression?
2. What criteria did you use to make the judgment?
3. After getting to know the person, did you find that your first impression was incorrect?

Student Instructions for Learning Stations

At the learning stations, you will analyze a story for the usage of plot, characterization, and dialogue. Discuss your answers with other team members after completing each activity.

Closure: Reflection

The following questions can be used to stimulate discussion or as a journaling activity.
1. What is the purpose of dialogue in a story?
2. Who is the protagonist and antagonist in your favorite novel?
3. What character traits would you use to describe yourself?

Name: _____ Date: _____

Station One: Plot

Plot is the sequence of events in a story. In most stories, the main character is confronted with a conflict. The plot moves forward as the main character tries to solve the conflict. The story ends with the resolution of the conflict.

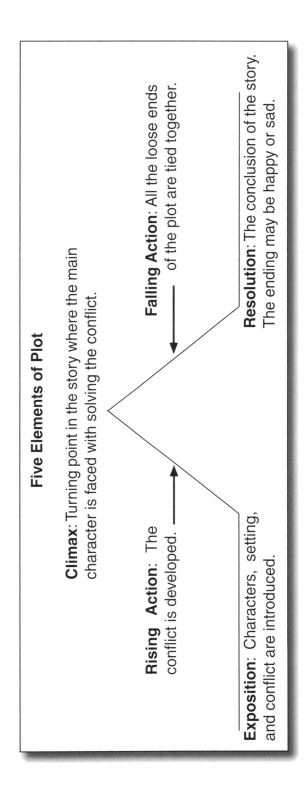

Five Elements of Plot

Climax: Turning point in the story where the main character is faced with solving the conflict.

Falling Action: All the loose ends of the plot are tied together.

Rising Action: The conflict is developed.

Resolution: The conclusion of the story. The ending may be happy or sad.

Exposition: Characters, setting, and conflict are introduced.

Directions: Fill in each element of plot listed in the chart for the story *Little Red Riding Hood.*

Exposition	Rising Action	Climax	Falling Action	Resolution

Name: _____   Date: _____

Station Two: Character Traits

In order to get to know the characters in a story, you need to pay attention to details. The author reveals traits in a description of the character's appearance, actions, emotions, and words they speak. If the author writes that the main character "has a sunny nature," the author means that the character is happy.

Directions: Read the story *Little Red Riding Hood*. In the graphic organizers, list three character traits for the wolf and three for *Little Red Riding Hood*. Cite textual evidence to support your decisions. If you need help, use the Examples of Character Traits handout.

Little Red Riding Hood	Character Trait Revealed by . . .
Trait	Cite textual evidence.
Trait	Cite textual evidence.
Trait	Cite textual evidence.

Mr. Wolf	Character Trait Revealed by . . .
Trait	Cite textual evidence.
Trait	Cite textual evidence.
Trait	Cite textual evidence.

Name: _____ Date: _____

Station Three: Character Types

Types of Characters

- **Dynamic Character:** undergoes a change usually brought about by the resolution of the conflict or the result of having faced a crisis
- **Static Character:** does not change or evolve
- **Round Character:** easy to identify their personality, physical, and emotional traits
- **Flat Character:** opposite of a round character; not well developed
- **Protagonist:** the main character, usually the hero of the story who resolves the conflict created by the antagonist
- **Antagonist:** usually the villain of the story who provides an obstacle for the protagonist

Directions: Read the story *Little Red Riding Hood*. Determine the character type for each character listed in the chart below and cite evidence to support your decision. A character may be a combination of more than one type.

Character	Character Type(s)	How Do You Know?
Little Red Riding Hood		
Mr. Wolf		
Mother		

Name: _____ Date: _____

Station Four: Analyzing Dialogue

Dialogue is the words spoken between characters in literature. Authors use dialogue to reveal the personality of characters, create conflict, or move the action of the story forward.

An author can create two types of dialogue: inner dialogue or outer dialogue.
- Inner dialogue is the words spoken by a character to himself/herself.
- Outer dialogue is the conversation spoken between characters.

Directions: Read the dialogue in the box below and answer the following questions.

> Little Red Riding Hood wandered from her path and was stooping to pick a flower when from behind her a gruff voice said, "Good morning, Little Red Riding Hood." Little Red Riding Hood turned around and saw a great big wolf, but Little Red Riding Hood did not know what a wicked beast the wolf was, so she was not afraid.
> "What have you in that basket, Little Red Riding Hood?"
> "Eggs and butter and cake, Mr. Wolf."
> "Where are you going with them, Little Red Riding Hood?"
> "I am going to my grandmother, who is ill, Mr. Wolf."
> "Where does your grandmother live, Little Red Riding Hood?"
> "Along that path, past the wild rose bushes, then through the gate at the end of the wood, Mr. Wolf."
> Then Mr. Wolf again said "Good morning" and set off, and Little Red Riding Hood again went in search of wild flowers.

1. What type of dialogue did the author use? How do you know?

   _____

   _____

2. What does the dialogue tell you about the two characters? Cite textual evidence from the passage to support your answer.

   _____

   _____

   _____

3. How does the dialogue move the plot forward? Cite textual evidence from the passage to support your answer.

   _____

   _____

   _____

Little Red Riding Hood

There was once a sweet little maid who lived with her father and mother in a pretty little cottage at the edge of the village. At the further end of the wood was another pretty cottage and in it lived her grandmother.

Everybody loved this little girl, her grandmother perhaps loved her most of all and gave her a great many pretty things. Once she gave her a red cloak with a hood which she always wore, so people called her Little Red Riding Hood.

One morning Little Red Riding Hood's mother said, "Put on your things and go to see your grandmother. She has been ill; take along this basket for her. I have put in it eggs, butter and cake, and other dainties."

It was a bright and sunny morning. Red Riding Hood was so happy that at first she wanted to dance through the wood[s]. All around her grew pretty wild flowers which she loved so well, and she stopped to pick a bunch for her grandmother.

Little Red Riding Hood wandered from her path and was stooping to pick a flower when from behind her a gruff voice said, "Good morning, Little Red Riding Hood." Little Red Riding Hood turned around and saw a great big wolf, but Little Red Riding Hood did not know what a wicked beast the wolf was, so she was not afraid.

"What have you in that basket, Little Red Riding Hood?"

"Eggs and butter and cake, Mr. Wolf."

"Where are you going with them, Little Red Riding Hood?"

"I am going to my grandmother, who is ill, Mr. Wolf."

"Where does your grandmother live, Little Red Riding Hood?"

"Along that path, past the wild rose bushes, then through the gate at the end of the wood, Mr. Wolf."

Then Mr. Wolf again said "Good morning" and set off, and Little Red Riding Hood again went in search of wild flowers.

Little Red Riding Hood (cont.)

At last he reached the porch covered with flowers and knocked at the door of the cottage.

"Who is there?" called the grandmother.

"Little Red Riding Hood," said the wicked wolf.

"Press the latch, open the door, and walk in," said the grandmother.

The wolf pressed the latch, and walked in where the grandmother lay in bed. He made one jump at her, but she jumped out of bed into a closet. Then the wolf put on the cap which she had dropped and crept under the bedclothes.

In a short while Little Red Riding Hood knocked at the door, and walked in, saying, "Good morning, Grandmother, I have brought you eggs, butter and cake, and here is a bunch of flowers I gathered in the wood." As she came nearer the bed she said, "What big ears you have, Grandmother."

"All the better to hear you with, my dear."

"What big eyes you have, Grandmother."

"All the better to see you with, my dear."

"But, Grandmother, what a big nose you have."

"All the better to smell with, my dear."

"But, Grandmother, what a big mouth you have."

"All the better to eat you up with, my dear," he said as he sprang at Little Red Riding Hood.

Just at that moment Little Red Riding Hood's father was passing the cottage and heard her scream. He rushed in and with his axe chopped off Mr. Wolf's head.

Everybody was happy that Little Red Riding Hood had escaped the wolf. Then Little Red Riding Hood's father carried her home and they lived happily ever after.

[Excerpted from *Children's Hour with Red Riding Hood and Other Stories* edited by Watty Piper, 1922]

Examples of Character Traits

adaptable	discouraged	impulsive	reserved
adventurous	dishonest	incompetent	respectful
affectionate	disrespectful	indecisive	responsible
afraid	dreamer	independent	romantic
aggressive	eager	insecure	rude
ambitious	easy-going	intelligent	ruthless
angry	eloquent	inventive	sarcastic
annoyed	embarrassed	irritable	scared
apologetic	encouraging	jealous	secretive
argumentative	energetic	jovial	self-centered
arrogant	expert	lazy	selfish
awkward	faithful	leadership	sensitive
bored	fearless	light-hearted	serious
bossy	fidgety	logical	shrewd
brave	fierce	lonely	shy
calm	flamboyant	lovable	silly
capable	flexible	loyal	sly
careless	foolish	malicious	smart
cautious	friendly	mean	sneaky
charming	frustrated	meek	spoiled
cheerful	funny	mischievous	squeamish
clever	furious	mysterious	stingy
cold-hearted	generous	nagging	strong
compassionate	gentle	naïve	stubborn
compulsive	giving	nervous	studious
conceited	glamorous	obedient	successful
concerned	gloomy	obnoxious	sympathetic
confident	grateful	observant	talented
confused	greedy	optimistic	thankful
considerate	grouchy	patient	thoughtful
consistent	gullible	patriotic	thrifty
controlling	happy	perceptive	timid
cooperative	hard-working	persevering	trusting
courageous	hateful	persistent	trustworthy
cowardly	helpful	persuasive	unfriendly
crafty	hesitant	picky	unhappy
creative	honest	polite	wise
cruel	hopeful	popular	witty
curious	hospitable	practical	
demanding	humble	proud	
dependable	immature	rash	
determined	impatient	reliable	

Teacher Page

Unit: Alliteration and Rhyme

Goal: Students will be able to recognize the use of alliteration and rhyme in poetry

Common Core State Standards (CCSS):

6th Grade	7th Grade	8th Grade
RL.6.4. Determine the meaning of words and phrases as they are used in a text, including figurative and connotative meanings; analyze the impact of a specific word choice on meaning and tone.	RL.7.4. Determine the meaning of words and phrases as they are used in a text, including figurative and connotative meanings; analyze the impact of rhymes and other repetitions of sounds (e.g., alliteration) on a specific verse or stanza of a poem or section of a story or drama.	RL.8.4. Determine the meaning of words and phrases as they are used in a text, including figurative and connotative meanings; analyze the impact of specific word choices on meaning and tone, including analogies or allusions to other texts.

© Copyright 2010. National Governors Association Center for Best Practices and Council of Chief State School Officers. All rights reserved.

Materials List/Setup

Station 1: Alliteration (Activity); "A Tale With a Moral" (Handout)
Station 2: Word Meaning (Activity); Dictionary (online or print)
Station 3: Rhyme Scheme (Activity); assortment of poetry books
Station 4: Internal Rhyme (Activity); variety of highlighter pens

Activity: one copy per student
Handout: one copy per each student in a group

Opening Activity and Discussion Questions (Teacher-Directed)

1. What is a moral?
2. What are some famous quotes with a moral (e.g., The early bird catches the worm)?
3. Simple Simon and Humpty Dumpty are two characters from Mother Goose Rhymes. Which name is an example of alliteration and which is an example of rhyme?
4. Why is rhyme used in poetry?
5. Why is alliteration used in poetry?

Student Instructions for Learning Stations

At the learning stations, you will analyze poetry for the use of alliteration, rhyme, and rhyme scheme. The activities will help you determine why certain words were used and the impact the words have on meaning and tone. Discuss your answers with other team members after completing each activity.

Closure: Reflection

The following questions can be used to stimulate discussion or as a journaling activity.
1. Do you like to read poems that rhyme?
2. Do you use rhyme or alliteration in poems you create? Why?
3. Do you find it easier to remember lines from poems that contain rhyme or alliteration?

Name: _____ Date: _____

Station One: Alliteration

Directions: Locate four examples of alliteration used in the poem "A Tale with a Moral" by Burges Johnson. What impact do the words have on the tone of the poem? Record your answers in the graphic organizer. Then answer the question below.

Examples of Alliteration	Tone

What impact does the word choice "tragedy" have on the meaning of the following lines?

*"And the glade is stiller than still can be
At thought of the coming **tragedy**."*

_____

_____

_____

Name: _____　　　　Date: _____

Station Two: Word Meaning

Directions: Read the following lines from the poem "The Gnu Wooing" by Burges Johnson. What do you think the bold words mean? What are the dictionary definitions of the bold words? What is the impact or tone of each bold word? Record your answers in the graphic organizer.

Said he: "If guests you would **eschew**,
I'll say **adieu** without **ado**;
But let me add I knew your dad:
I'm on page two, the Gnu's 'Who's Who.'"
"Forgive," she cried, "the snub I threw!
I feared you were some **parvegnu***!

*Parvegnu is an example of word play and was created by mixing the words *parvenu* and *gnu*.

Word	What You Think the Word Means	Dictionary Meaning
eschew		
adieu		
ado		
parvenu		

What is the impact of the author's word choice on tone? Cite textual evidence to support your answer.

_____

_____

_____

_____

Name: _____   Date: _____

Station Three: Rhyme Scheme

The **rhyme scheme** of a poem is the pattern of rhyme at the end of each line of a stanza or poem. To be a scheme, the pattern must be continued throughout the entire poem. Capital letters are used to mark the pattern of the rhyme.

Examples of Patterns

Pattern AABB
Twinkle, twinkle, little star, **A**
How I wonder what you are! **A**
Up above the world so high, **B**
Like a diamond in the sky. **B**

Pattern ABCB
Jack Sprat could eat no fat, **A**
His wife could eat no lean, **B**
And so, betwixt them both, **C**
They licked the platter clean. **B**

Directions: Locate a poem for each rhyme scheme in column one. In the graphic organizer, list the title of the poem, write the first stanza, and then mark the rhyme scheme.

Rhyme Scheme	Title of the Poem	First Stanza
ABAB		
AABB		
AABBCC		

Name: _____   Date: _____

Station Four: Internal Rhyme

Internal rhyme is when two or more words within the same line rhyme, usually a word in the middle with the end word. The rhyming could also occur with the end word of one line and one or more of the middle words in the next line.

> **Example:** 'Twas a gloomy **glade** 'mid the lowering **shade**
> Burges Johnson, "A Tale with a Moral"
>
> **Example:** For we cannot help **agreeing** that no living human **being**
> Ever yet was blessed with **seeing** bird above his chamber door
> Edgar Allan Poe, "The Raven"

Directions: Highlight the internal rhyme in the following stanzas.

1. There was a lovely lady Gnu
   Who browsed beneath a spreading yew.
   Its stately height was her delight:
   A truly cooling shade it threw.
   Upon it little tendrils grew
   Which gave her gentle joy to chew.
   Yet oft she sighed, a-gazing wide,
   And wished she knew another Gnu
   (Some newer Gnu beneath the yew
   To tell her tiny troubles to.)

(Excerpt from "The Gnu Wooing" by Burges Johnson)

2. Deep into that darkness peering, long I stood there wondering, fearing,
   Doubting, dreaming dreams no mortal ever dared to dream before;
   But the silence was unbroken, and the darkness gave no token,
   And the only word there spoken was the whispered word, 'Lenore!'
   This I whispered, and an echo murmured back the word, 'Lenore!'
   Merely this and nothing more.

   (Excerpt from "The Raven" by Edgar Allen Poe)

3. The bridegroom's doors are opened wide,
   And I am next of kin;
   The guests are met, the feast is set:
   Mayst hear the merry din.

   (Excerpt from "The Rime of the Ancient Mariner" by Samuel Taylor Coleridge)

A Tale With a Moral

'Twas a gloomy glade 'mid the lowering shade
Of a forest dank and dark;
And every decent creature slept,
For the gray of dawn had scarcely crept
O'er the morning sky. But hark!
Amid the silence there may be heard
The drowsy chirp of the Early Bird.

To the ground he flits, where he lightly sits,
Then hops with a movement gay.
"Cheep-cheep, te-whit!" and he flaps his wings;
"Oh, I am the Early Bird," he sings,
And also "Tu-lu-ra-lay!"
But though he carols it through and through,
His joyful warble does not ring true!

Lo, a twig that lies beneath his eyes
Of a sudden appears to squirm!
And there comes from under his very feet
A faint fine sound that I can't repeat—
The voice of the Early Worm!
And the glade is stiller than still can be
At thought of the coming tragedy.

"It is up to me," sobbed the Worm, "to flee,
Were I not such a sleepy thing!"
But the Bird was wabbly on his feet;
"I'm far too drowsy," he sighed, "to eat!"
And his head fell under his wing.
And, sweetly mingled, there soon were heard
The snores of the Worm and the Early Bird.
                    —Burges Johnson

(From *Beastly Rhymes* by Burges Johnson, 1906)

Teacher Page

Unit: Point of View

Goal: Students will be able to identify points of view and analyze how points of view can differ between characters and how it can be used to create effects, such as suspense and humor.

Common Core State Standards (CCSS):

6th Grade	7th Grade	8th Grade
RL.6.6. Explain how an author develops the point of view of the narrator or speaker in a text.	RL.7.6. Analyze how an author develops and contrasts the points of view of different characters or narrators in a text.	RL.8.6. Analyze how differences in the points of view of the characters and the audience or reader (e.g., created through the use of dramatic irony) create such effects as suspense or humor.

© Copyright 2010. National Governors Association Center for Best Practices and Council of Chief State School Officers. All rights reserved.

Materials List/Setup

Station 1: Narrative Point of View (Activity); *The Jungle Book* (Handout)
Station 2: Character's Point of View (Activity); *The Jungle Book* (Handout)
Station 3: Mood (Activity)
Station 4: Comparing Points of View (Activity); *The Jungle Book* (Handout)

Activity: one copy per student
Handout: one copy per each student in a group

Opening Activity and Discussion Questions (Teacher-Directed)

1. Have you and your friend ever read the same book, but you liked the book and your friend did not like the book?
2. Why did you and your friend have different points of view about the book?

Student Instructions for Learning Stations

At the learning stations, you will read a passage from the book *The Jungle Book* by Rudyard Kipling. You will identify points of view and analyze how points of view can differ between characters and how it can be used to create effects, such as suspense and humor. Discuss your answers with other team members after completing each activity.

Closure: Reflection

The following questions can be used to stimulate discussion or as a journaling activity.
1. Why do authors write narratives from different points of view?
2. How does an author develop a character's personal point of view?

Name: _____ Date: _____

Station One: Narrative Point of View

When you determine who is telling a story, you have discovered the **narrative point of view**.

Types of Narrative Point of View

First-person: One of the characters tells the story from his or her own perspective.
  First-person uses the pronouns "I" or "my."

Second-person: The narrator is telling the story to the reader as if the reader were a character.
  Second-person uses the pronouns "you" and "your."

Third-person: The narrator is someone outside the story.
  Third-person uses the pronouns "he," "she," "they," and "it."

Directions: Read the passage from *The Jungle Book* and then answer the questions.

1. What type of narrative point of view did the author use to write the passage? Cite textual evidence to support your answer.

   _____

   _____

   _____

   _____

   _____

   _____

2. Why do you think Kipling chose this point of view to write *The Jungle Book*?

   _____

   _____

   _____

   _____

   _____

   _____

Name: _____ Date: _____

Station Two: Character's Point of View

A **character's personal point of view** is how that character feels about a person or situation. A character shows a positive point of view if the author uses word choices such as happiness, pride, hope, and joy. A character has a negative point of view if the author uses word choices such as sorrow, shame, fear, and anger. A neutral point of view is when the character's opinion is not revealed by word choice.

Directions: Read the passage *The Jungle Book*. Complete the graphic organizer by identifying each character's point of view (positive or negative) toward Mowgli. Cite textual evidence to support your answer.

Character	Character's Point of View Toward Mowgli	Purpose
Mother Wolf		
Baloo		
Shere Khan		

Name: _____ Date: _____

Station Three: Mood

Mood is the feeling the reader gets from reading the author's words.

Directions: Read the two passages from *The Jungle Book* and then answer the questions.

Passage One

The bushes rustled a little in the thicket, and Father Wolf dropped with his haunches under him, ready for his leap. Then, if you had been watching, you would have seen the most wonderful thing in the world—the wolf checked in mid-spring. He made his bound before he saw what it was he was jumping at, and then he tried to stop himself. The result was that he shot up straight into the air for four or five feet, landing almost where he left ground.

Directly in front of him, holding on by a low branch, stood a naked brown baby who could just walk—as soft and as dimpled a little atom as ever came to a wolf's cave at night. He looked up into Father Wolf's face, and laughed.

(Excerpt from *The Jungle Book* by Rudyard Kipling)

Passage Two

A black shadow dropped down into the circle. It was Bagheera the Black Panther, inky black all over, but with the panther markings showing up in certain lights like the pattern of watered silk. Everybody knew Bagheera, and nobody cared to cross his path; for he was as cunning as Tabaqui, as bold as the wild buffalo, and as reckless as the wounded elephant. But he had a voice as soft as wild honey dripping from a tree, and a skin softer than down.

"O Akela, and ye the Free People," he purred, "I have no right in your assembly, but the Law of the Jungle says that if there is a doubt which is not a killing matter in regard to a new cub, the life of that cub may be bought at a price. And the Law does not say who may or may not pay that price. Am I right?"

"Good! Good!" said the young wolves, who are always hungry. "Listen to Bagheera. The cub can be bought for a price. It is the Law."

(Excerpt from *The Jungle Book* by Rudyard Kipling)

---

1. What is the mood of Passage One? How do you know?

   _____

   _____

2. What is the mood of Passage Two? How do you know?

   _____

Name: _____   Date: _____

Station Four: Comparing Points of View

Directions: Choose two characters from the passage, *The Jungle Book*. Use the Venn diagram to compare and contrast the character's feelings about Mowgli.

Character's Points of View

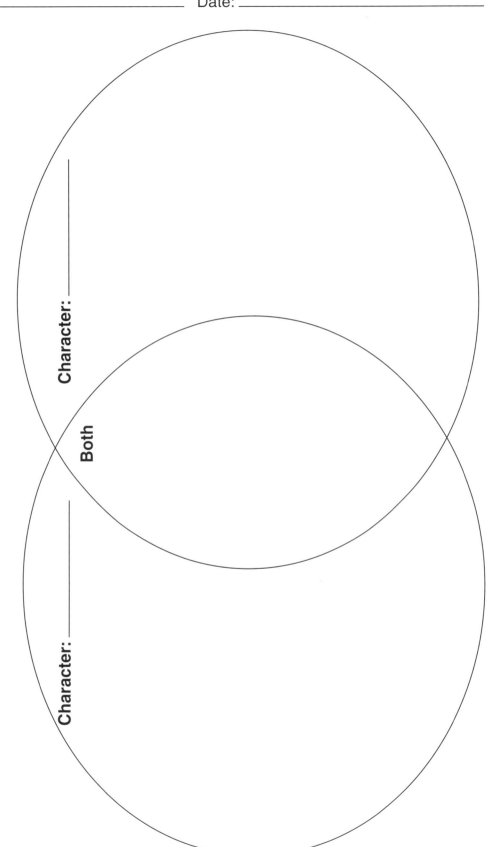

Character: _____

Both

Character: _____

The Jungle Book

The bushes rustled a little in the thicket, and Father Wolf dropped with his haunches under him, ready for his leap. Then, if you had been watching, you would have seen the most wonderful thing in the world—the wolf checked in mid-spring. He made his bound before he saw what it was he was jumping at, and then he tried to stop himself. The result was that he shot up straight into the air for four or five feet, landing almost where he left ground.

"Man!" he snapped. "A man's cub. Look!"

Directly in front of him, holding on by a low branch, stood a naked brown baby who could just walk—as soft and as dimpled a little atom as ever came to a wolf's cave at night. He looked up into Father Wolf's face, and laughed.

"Is that a man's cub?" said Mother Wolf. "I have never seen one. Bring it here."

A Wolf accustomed to moving his own cubs can, if necessary, mouth an egg without breaking it, and though Father Wolf's jaws closed right on the child's back not a tooth even scratched the skin as he laid it down among the cubs.

"How little! How naked, and—how bold!" said Mother Wolf softly. The baby was pushing his way between the cubs to get close to the warm hide. "Ahai! He is taking his meal with the others. And so this is a man's cub. Now, was there ever a wolf that could boast of a man's cub among her children?"

"I have heard now and again of such a thing, but never in our Pack or in my time," said Father Wolf. "He is altogether without hair, and I could kill him with a touch of my foot. But see, he looks up and is not afraid."

The moonlight was blocked out of the mouth of the cave, for Shere Khan's great square head and shoulders were thrust into the entrance. Tabaqui, behind him, was squeaking: "My lord, my lord, it went in here!"

"Shere Khan does us great honor," said Father Wolf, but his eyes were very angry. "What does Shere Khan need?"

"My quarry. A man's cub went this way," said Shere Khan. "Its parents have run off. Give it to me."

Shere Khan had jumped at a woodcutter's campfire, as Father Wolf had said, and was furious from the pain of his burned feet. But Father Wolf knew that the mouth of the cave was too narrow for a tiger to come in by. Even where he was, Shere Khan's shoulders and forepaws were cramped for want of room, as a man's would be if he tried to fight in a barrel.

"The Wolves are a free people," said Father Wolf. "They take orders from the Head of the Pack, and not from any striped cattle-killer. The man's cub is ours—to kill if we choose."

"Ye choose and ye do not choose! What talk is this of choosing? By the bull that I killed, am I to stand nosing into your dog's den for my fair dues? It is I, Shere Khan, who speak!"

The Jungle Book (cont.)

The tiger's roar filled the cave with thunder. Mother Wolf shook herself clear of the cubs and sprang forward, her eyes, like two green moons in the darkness, facing the blazing eyes of Shere Khan.

"And it is I, Raksha [The Demon], who answers. The man's cub is mine, Lungri—mine to me! He shall not be killed. He shall live to run with the Pack and to hunt with the Pack; and in the end, look you, hunter of little naked cubs—frog-eater—fish-killer—he shall hunt thee! Now get hence, or by the Sambhur that I killed (I eat no starved cattle), back thou goest to thy mother, burned beast of the jungle, lamer than ever thou camest into the world! Go!"

Father Wolf looked on amazed. He had almost forgotten the days when he won Mother Wolf in fair fight from five other wolves, when she ran in the Pack and was not called The Demon for compliment's sake. Shere Khan might have faced Father Wolf, but he could not stand up against Mother Wolf, for he knew that where he was she had all the advantage of the ground, and would fight to the death. So he backed out of the cave mouth growling, and when he was clear he shouted:

"Each dog barks in his own yard! We will see what the Pack will say to this fostering of man-cubs. The cub is mine, and to my teeth he will come in the end, O bush-tailed thieves!"

Mother Wolf threw herself down panting among the cubs, and Father Wolf said to her gravely: "Shere Khan speaks this much truth. The cub must be shown to the Pack. Wilt thou still keep him, Mother?"

"Keep him!" she gasped. "He came naked, by night, alone and very hungry; yet he was not afraid! Look, he has pushed one of my babes to one side already. And that lame butcher would have killed him and would have run off to the Waingunga while the villagers here hunted through all our lairs in revenge! Keep him? Assuredly I will keep him. Lie still, little frog. O thou Mowgli—for Mowgli the Frog I will call thee—the time will come when thou wilt hunt Shere Khan as he has hunted thee."

"But what will our Pack say?" said Father Wolf.

The Law of the Jungle lays down very clearly that any wolf may, when he marries, withdraw from the Pack he belongs to. But as soon as his cubs are old enough to stand on their feet he must bring them to the Pack Council, which is generally held once a month at full moon, in order that the other wolves may identify them. After that inspection the cubs are free to run where they please, and until they have killed their first buck no excuse is accepted if a grown wolf of the Pack kills one of them. The punishment is death where the murderer can be found; and if you think for a minute you will see that this must be so.

Father Wolf waited till his cubs could run a little, and then on the night of the Pack Meeting took them and Mowgli and Mother Wolf to the Council Rock—a hilltop covered with stones and boulders where a hundred wolves could hide. Akela, the great gray Lone Wolf, who led all the Pack by strength and cunning, lay out at full length on his rock, and below him sat forty or more wolves of every size and color, from badger-colored veterans who could handle a buck alone to

The Jungle Book (cont.)

young black three-year-olds who thought they could. The Lone Wolf had led them for a year now. He had fallen twice into a wolf trap in his youth, and once he had been beaten and left for dead; so he knew the manners and customs of men. There was very little talking at the Rock. The cubs tumbled over each other in the center of the circle where their mothers and fathers sat, and now and again a senior wolf would go quietly up to a cub, look at him carefully, and return to his place on noiseless feet. Sometimes a mother would push her cub far out into the moonlight to be sure that he had not been overlooked. Akela from his rock would cry: "Ye know the Law—ye know the Law. Look well, O Wolves!" And the anxious mothers would take up the call: "Look—look well, O Wolves!"

At last—and Mother Wolf's neck bristles lifted as the time came—Father Wolf pushed "Mowgli the Frog," as they called him, into the center, where he sat laughing and playing with some pebbles that glistened in the moonlight.

Akela never raised his head from his paws, but went on with the monotonous cry: "Look well!" A muffled roar came up from behind the rocks—the voice of Shere Khan crying: "The cub is mine. Give him to me. What have the Free People to do with a man's cub?" Akela never even twitched his ears. All he said was: "Look well, O Wolves! What have the Free People to do with the orders of any save the Free People? Look well!"

There was a chorus of deep growls, and a young wolf in his fourth year flung back Shere Khan's question to Akela: "What have the Free People to do with a man's cub?" Now, the Law of the Jungle lays down that if there is any dispute as to the right of a cub to be accepted by the Pack, he must be spoken for by at least two members of the Pack who are not his father and mother.

"Who speaks for this cub?" said Akela. "Among the Free People who speaks?" There was no answer and Mother Wolf got ready for what she knew would be her last fight, if things came to fighting.

Then the only other creature who is allowed at the Pack Council—Baloo, the sleepy brown bear who teaches the wolf cubs the Law of the Jungle: old Baloo, who can come and go where he pleases because he eats only nuts and roots and honey—rose upon his hind quarters and grunted.

"The man's cub—the man's cub?" he said. "I speak for the man's cub. There is no harm in a man's cub. I have no gift of words, but I speak the truth. Let him run with the Pack, and be entered with the others. I myself will teach him."

"We need yet another," said Akela. "Baloo has spoken, and he is our teacher for the young cubs. Who speaks besides Baloo?"

A black shadow dropped down into the circle. It was Bagheera the Black Panther, inky black all over, but with the panther markings showing up in certain lights like the pattern of watered silk. Everybody knew Bagheera, and nobody cared to cross his path; for he was as cunning as Tabaqui, as bold as the wild buffalo, and as reckless as the wounded elephant. But he had a voice as soft as wild honey dripping from a tree, and a skin softer than down.

The Jungle Book (cont.)

"O Akela, and ye the Free People," he purred, "I have no right in your assembly, but the Law of the Jungle says that if there is a doubt which is not a killing matter in regard to a new cub, the life of that cub may be bought at a price. And the Law does not say who may or may not pay that price. Am I right?"

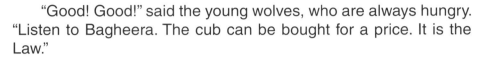

"Good! Good!" said the young wolves, who are always hungry. "Listen to Bagheera. The cub can be bought for a price. It is the Law."

"Knowing that I have no right to speak here, I ask your leave."

"Speak then," cried twenty voices.

"To kill a naked cub is shame. Besides, he may make better sport for you when he is grown. Baloo has spoken in his behalf. Now to Baloo's word I will add one bull, and a fat one, newly killed, not half a mile from here, if ye will accept the man's cub according to the Law. Is it difficult?"

There was a clamor of scores of voices, saying: "What matter? He will die in the winter rains. He will scorch in the sun. What harm can a naked frog do us? Let him run with the Pack. Where is the bull, Bagheera? Let him be accepted." And then came Akela's deep bay, crying: "Look well—look well, O Wolves!"

Mowgli was still deeply interested in the pebbles, and he did not notice when the wolves came and looked at him one by one. At last they all went down the hill for the dead bull, and only Akela, Bagheera, Baloo, and Mowgli's own wolves were left. Shere Khan roared still in the night, for he was very angry that Mowgli had not been handed over to him.

"Ay, roar well," said Bagheera, under his whiskers, "for the time will come when this naked thing will make thee roar to another tune, or I know nothing of man."

"It was well done," said Akela. "Men and their cubs are very wise. He may be a help in time."

"Truly, a help in time of need; for none can hope to lead the Pack forever," said Bagheera.

Akela said nothing. He was thinking of the time that comes to every leader of every pack when his strength goes from him and he gets feebler and feebler, till at last he is killed by the wolves and a new leader comes up—to be killed in his turn.

"Take him away," he said to Father Wolf, "and train him as befits one of the Free People." And that is how Mowgli was entered into the Seeonee Wolf Pack for the price of a bull and on Baloo's good word.

(Excerpt from *The Jungle Book* by Rudyard Kipling)

Teacher Page

Unit: Poetry

Goal: Students will be able to interpret the literary language used in poetry.

Common Core State Standards (CCSS):

6th Grade	7th Grade	8th Grade
RL.6.9. Compare and contrast texts in different forms or genres (e.g., stories and poems; historical novels and fantasy stories) in terms of their approaches to similar themes and topics.	RL.7.9. Compare and contrast a fictional portrayal of a time, place, or character and a historical account of the same period as a means of understanding how authors of fiction use or alter history.	RL.8.9. Analyze how a modern work of fiction draws on themes, patterns of events, or character types from myths, traditional stories, or religious works such as the Bible, including describing how the material is rendered new.

© Copyright 2010. National Governors Association Center for Best Practices and Council of Chief State School Officers. All rights reserved.

Materials List/Setup

Station 1: Extended Metaphor Poem (Activity); "O Captain! My Captain!" (Handout)
Station 2: Poems: Compare and Contrast (Activity); "O Captain! My Captain!" (Handout);
       "The Martyr" (Handout)
Station 3: Citing Textual Evidence (Activity); "O Captain! My Captain!" (Handout)
Station 4: Literary Devices (Activity); "O Captain! My Captain!" (Handout)

Activity: one copy per student
Handout: one copy per each student in a group

Opening Activity and Discussion Questions (Teacher-Directed)

1. What do you know about the American Civil War?
2. What do you know about the assassination of President Abraham Lincoln?
3. What is an extended metaphor poem?

Student Instructions for Learning Stations

At the learning stations, you will analyze two poems with the same theme. Discuss your answers with other team members after completing each activity.

Closure: Reflection

The following questions can be used to stimulate discussion or as a journaling activity.
1. How can you tell the poem "O Captain! My Captain" is an example of an extended metaphor poem?
2. What is the difference between reading Walt Whitman's poem about Abraham Lincoln and reading about Lincoln in a textbook?

Name: _____ Date: _____

Station One: Extended Metaphor Poem

A **metaphor** is a comparison of two like or unlike things.

Example: The **snow** is a **blanket** covering the countryside.

Snow and a **blanket** are being compared. They are alike because they both cover something.

An **extended metaphor poem** takes a metaphor and compares it throughout the poem. "O Captain! My Captain!" is an extended metaphor poem. Walt Whitman wrote this poem as a tribute to President Abraham Lincoln, who was assassinated just before the end of the Civil War.

Directions: Read the poem "O Captain! My Captain!" and complete the chart below.

Extended Metaphor	Meaning
"the captain"	
"the trip"	
"the vessel"	
"the ship has weathered every rack"	
"the prize we sought is won"	

Name: _____ Date: _____

Station Two: Compare and Contrast

Walt Whitman wrote the poem "O Captain! My Captain!" after the assassination of Abraham Lincoln in 1865. Herman Melville also wrote a poem about President Lincoln's death. The name of Melville's poem is "The Martyr."

Directions: Use the Venn diagram to compare and contrast the tone of the poem "O Captain! My Captain!" to the tone of the poem "The Martyr."

Tone

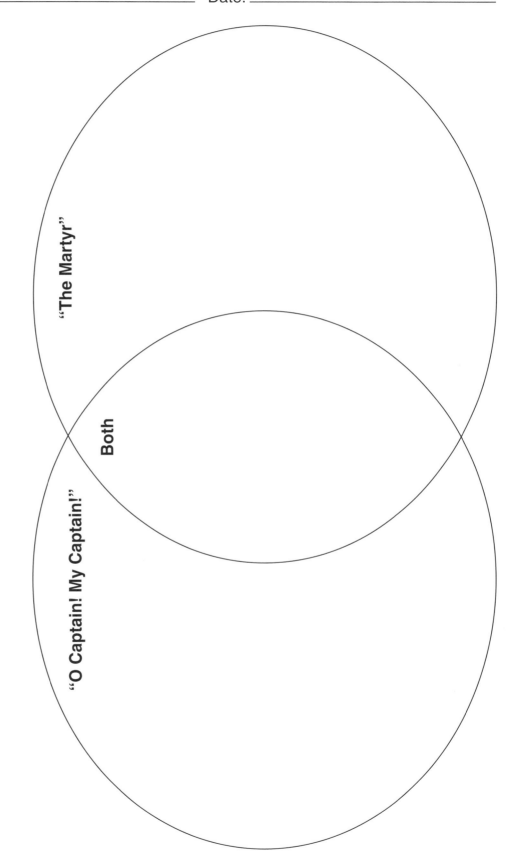

"The Martyr"

Both

"O Captain! My Captain!"

Name: _____ Date: _____

Station Three: Citing Textual Evidence

Directions: Read "O Captain! My Captain!" and answer the questions below.

1. What is the theme of the poem? _____

   _____

   _____

2. Who is the intended audience for the poem? _____

   _____

   _____

3. Describe the attitude of the poem's narrator toward President
   Lincoln. Cite evidence from the poem to support your answer.

   _____

   _____

   _____

   _____

4. Which side is the narrator most likely to have supported during the Civil War: the Union or
   Confederacy? Cite evidence from the poem to support your answer.

   _____

   _____

   _____

   _____

5. What can you infer about the Union victory from stanza two of the poem? Cite textual evidence to support your answer.

   _____

   _____

   _____

   _____

Name: _____   Date: _____

Station Four: Literary Devices

Directions: Read the poem "O Captain! My Captain!" and complete the chart.

Mood is how the poet makes you feel when you read his or her poems. Examples of words that describe mood are *frightening*, *mysterious*, *happy*, *sorrowful*, and *joyful*.	What is the mood of the poem? Cite textual evidence.
Tone is how the poet feels toward the topic. Examples of words that describe tone are *amused*, *angry*, *sad*, *serious*, *gloomy*, and *playful*.	What is the tone of the poem? Cite textual evidence.
Imagery is created by the words and phrases that appeal to the five senses.	Give two examples of imagery used in the poem. Cite textual evidence.
Author's Purpose is the reason an author writes on a specific topic.	What is the author's purpose for writing the poem? Cite textual evidence.

O Captain! My Captain!

Walt Whitman wrote the poem "O Captain! My Captain!" following the assassination of Abraham Lincoln in 1865. Whitman revised his poem several times. On February 9, 1888, Whitman wrote to a publisher about the errors to his poem that appeared in their anthology. He sent a correction sheet to the publisher. The poem below reflects Whitman's 1888 revisions. To view the primary source and read more about this story, go online to: The Library of Congress—American Memory Collection.

O Captain! My Captain!

O Captain! my Captain! our fearful trip is done;
The ship has weather'd every rack, the prize we sought is won;
The port is near, the bells I hear, the people all exulting,
While follow eyes the steady keel, the vessel grim and daring.
But O heart! heart! heart!
O the bleeding drops of red!
Where on the deck my captain lies,
Fallen cold and dead.

O Captain! my Captain! rise up and hear the bells;
Rise up—for you the flag is flung—for you the bugle trills:
For you bouquets and ribbon'd wreaths—for you the shores a-crowding:
For you they call, the swaying mass, their eager faces turning;
Here Captain! dear father!
This arm beneath your head;
It is some dream that on the deck
You've fallen cold and dead.

My Captain does not answer, his lips are pale and still:
My father does not feel my arm, he has no pulse nor will.
The ship is anchor'd safe and sound, its voyage closed and done:
From fearful trip the victor ship comes in with object won;
Exult, O shores, and ring, O bells!
But I, with silent tread,
Walk the deck my Captain lies
Fallen cold and dead.

—Walt Whitman

The Martyr

THE MARTYR

Indicative of the passion of the people on the 15th of April, 1865.

Good Friday was the day
Of the prodigy and crime,
When they killed him in his pity,
When they killed him in his prime
Of clemency and calm—
When with yearning he was filled
To redeem the evil-willed,
And, though conqueror, be kind;
But they killed him in his kindness,
In their madness and their blindness,
And they killed him from behind.

There is sobbing of the strong,
And a pall upon the land;
But the People in their weeping
Bare the iron hand:
Beware the People weeping
When they bare the iron hand.

He lieth in his blood—
The father in his face;
They have killed him, the Forgiver—
The Avenger takes his place,
The Avenger wisely stern,
Who in righteousness shall do
What the heavens call him to,
And the parricides remand;
For they killed him in his kindness,
In their madness and their blindness,
And his blood is on their hand.

There is sobbing of the strong,
And a pall upon the land;
But the People in their weeping
Bare the iron hand:
Beware the People weeping
When they bare the iron hand.

—Herman Melville

Answer Keys

*If applicable, answers are provided.

Unit: Literature: Inferences and Evidence
Finding Evidence (p. 4)
Answers will vary but may include:
1. Buck did not read the newspapers, or he would have known that trouble was brewing, not alone for himself, but for every tide-water dog.
2. swam in the swimming tank; went hunting; took long rambles; lay at the Judge's feet before the roaring fire; carried the Judge's grandsons on his back; he was king over all creeping, crawling, flying things of Judge Miller's place, humans included; he had lived the life of a sated aristocrat
3. big house; wide cool veranda; spreading lawns; spacious scale; great stables; rows of vine-clad servants' cottages; demesne
4. father was a St. Bernard, mother was a Scotch shepherd dog.

Analyzing Text (p. 5)
Answers will vary but may include:
1. She was Hal's sister.
2. Yes, Hal and Charles followed the advice of Mercedes. "When they put a clothes-sack on the front of the sled, she suggested it should go on the back; and when they had put it on the back. . . she discovered overlooked articles which could abide nowhere else but in that very sack, and they unloaded again."
3. The campsite was a "slipshod and slovenly affair, tent half stretched, dishes unwashed," and it was all in a "disorder."
4. The dogs were "tired and weak," "jaded and tired," and "dead weary."
5. Charles and Hal "did not know how to do anything." Both of them "were slack in all things, without order or discipline." "It took them half the night to" make camp, and "half the morning to break that camp." They did not know how to pack a sled properly and had to stop and rearrange the load. "Some days they did not make ten miles. On other days they were unable to get started at all." They ran out of dog food.

Making a Comparison (p. 6)
Answers will vary but may include:
1. John Thornton played games; ideal master; treated the dogs "as if they were his own children"; kindly greetings; cheering words; would "sit down and talk"; took "Buck's head roughly between his hands," and rested "his head upon Buck's," then shake Buck "back and forth"
Buck adored John Thornton at a distance; "lie by the hour, at Thornton's feet, looking up into his face, dwelling upon it, studying it, following with keenest interest each fleeting expression, every movement or change of feature"; would follow at Thornton's heels. John Thornton had saved his life. "His love was expressed in adoration." He would watch Thornton's every move, and "follow at his heels."
2. John Thornton was the "ideal master." He treated Buck, like he did all his dogs, "like they were his own children."

Making Inferences (p. 7)
1. The call from the forest filled him with "a great unrest and strange desires. It caused him to feel a vague, sweet gladness, and he was aware of wild yearnings and stirrings for he knew not what."
2. The howl of the wolf was like the call of the forest that he had heard before, but this time it was more "distinct and definite." He felt that the wolf was his "wild brother."
3. Buck's internal conflict was the struggle between his desire to go with the wolf, his "wild brother," and his tie to stay with John Thornton.

Citing Textual Evidence (p. 8)
1. Buck knew John Thornton was dead because he "followed his trace into the water, from which no trace led away."
2. Buck was ready to obey the call because John Thornton was dead. "The last tie" to man "was broken."
3. He joined with the wolves in "howling at the moon." He ran with his "wild brother, yelping as he ran."

Unit: Plot, Setting, and Character
Plot (p. 15)

Exposition: Characters: Little Red Riding Hood, Mr. Wolf, Grandmother, Father, and Mother
Setting: the woods and grandmother's house
Conflict: Mr. Wolf tricks Little Red Riding Hood

Rising Action: Little Red Riding Hood gathers flowers while Mr. Wolf goes to grandmother's house and chases her into the closet.

Climax: Mr. Wolf tries to trick Little Red Riding Hood into thinking he is her grandmother. Little Red Riding Hood becomes suspicious. Mr. Wolf jumps out of the bed and tries to get Little Red Riding Hood.

Falling Action: Little Red Riding Hood's father arrives and chops off Mr. Wolf's head.

Resolution: Little Red Riding Hood's father carries her home, and they live happily ever after.

Character Traits (p. 16)

Little Red Riding Hood: sweet—"sweet little maid"
naïve—"Little Red Riding Hood did not know what a wicked beast Mr. Wolf was, so she was not afraid."
caring—"she stopped to pick a bunch for her grandmother."

Mr. Wolf: wicked: "said the wicked wolf."
gruff: "a gruff voice said"
cunning: "Then the wolf put on the cap which she had dropped and crept under the bedclothes."

Character Types (p. 17)

Little Red Riding Hood: protagonist: The entire story revolves around this character. The title of the story is "Little Red Riding Hood," which shows she is an important character.
round: Her appearance and personality are well-developed. She wore a red cloak with a hood. She is described as a sweet little girl. She is caring because she "stops to pick a bunch of flowers for her grandmother."

Mr. Wolf: antagonist: He is the villain of the story. He is described as wicked.
round: From the story, we know that he has a gruff voice, big ears, big nose, big mouth, and is wicked.

Mother: static: Mother is only in one paragraph of the story. Her character does not change or evolve.
flat: The story does not provide information about her appearance, personality, or emotions.

Analyzing Dialogue (p. 18)

1. outer dialogue—characters speak to each other
2. Little Red Riding Hood: The dialogue shows that Little Red Riding Hood was naïve. She "did not know what a wicked beast the wolf was, so she was not afraid." Also, in the dialogue, she tells Mr. Wolf how to get to her grandmother's house.
Mr. Wolf: In the dialogue, we can see that Mr. Wolf is inquisitive. He asks Little Red Riding Hood several questions, such as what is in her basket and "where are you going."
3. The plot is moved forward by Mr. Wolf asking Little Red Riding Hood where she is going. She responds, "Along that path, past the wild rose bushes, then through the gate at the end of the wood, Mr. Wolf." The author uses the dialogue to get Mr. Wolf to the grandmother's house.

Unit: Alliteration and Rhyme
Word Meaning (p. 24)

Answers will vary in column one.
eschew: to deliberately avoid; formal
adieu: goodbye; formal
ado: trouble or fuss; formal
parvenu: somebody of the lower class who has risen in rank or stature; dignified
Word Choice: The usage of words like eschew, adieu, ado, and parvenu sets a formal, dignified, upper-class tone.

Internal Rhyme (p. 26)

1. height-delight; sighed-wide; knew-Gnu; Gnu-yew-to
2. peering-fearing; unbroken-token-spoken
3. met-set

Unit: Point of View
Narrative Point of View (p. 29)
1. The story is told from a third-person point of view. (Textual evidence will vary.)
2. Third-person allows the reader to understand the perspectives of many characters.

Character's Point of View (p. 30)
Mother Wolf: positive (Textual evidence will vary.)
Baloo: positive (Textual evidence will vary.)
Shere Khan: negative (Textual evidence will vary.)

Unit: Poetry
Extended Metaphor Poem (p. 38)
1. President Abraham Lincoln
2. American Civil War
3. United States
4. The United States had weathered every adversity of the American Civil War.
5. Preservation of the Union

Compare and Contrast (p. 39)
"O Captain! My Captain!": The tone starts out happy then turns tragic. (Textual evidence may vary.)
Both: Both poems start out with one tone, then switches to another.
"The Martyr": Tone starts out sorrowful then turns fearful. (Textual evidence may vary.)

Citing Textual Evidence (p. 40)
1. death of President Abraham Lincoln
2. people who were mourning Lincoln's death
3. He was fond of Lincoln, because he calls him "dear father." He was respectful of Lincoln, because he refers to him as "Captain."
4. Union: The use of the word "we" in the line, "The ship has weathered every rack, the prize we sought is won".
5. The Union was glad the war was over and gave Lincoln the credit for the victory. This is shown by the use of the words "for you" before each of the listed accolades.

Literary Devices (p. 41)
Mood: Answers will vary.
Tone: The tone starts out happy then turns tragic. (Textual evidence may vary.)
Imagery: Answers will vary.
Author's Purpose: to pay tribute to President Abraham Lincoln (Textual evidence may vary.)